Inviting all the Ghosts to Dinner

Shaelyn Rhiannon

Dedication

This is for anyone who reads these poems and can relate to the sad ones. I'm sorry. You deserved better but you've figured out how to take care of yourself. I'm proud of you.

Contents

Note to readers

Hey everyone, this poetry collection does contain talk of mental illness and all the trials and tribulations that can come along with struggling with, in my case, anxiety, depression and ADHD.

I just wanted to include in here that if you struggle with your mental health, you are FAR from alone. I know it can feel like you are. I know due to our society you can feel a sense of shame. There is nothing to be ashamed of.

You are a beautiful person who has an abundance of worth. Never let anyone tell you differently. Please, take care of yourself and reach out to those who are qualified to help you, should you need it.

-Shaelyn

Inviting all the ghosts to dinner

The table is set.
Candles are lit.
A deep breath of smoky courage
Before it begins.

The opening of a heart.
The healing of a mind.

Countless ghosts in fancy clothes settle in.
Some are old friends, others are strangers.
Lessons learned over again.

These are my fantasies of a life.
Truths hidden in plain sight.
Chances that never played out right.

Memories divided into digestible bites.
People I loved.
People I hurt.
The fun I had numbing my heart.

All in a room.
Part of my story.

And as I enter, they all look up.
Smiling.
I've finally stopped running.

Ghost child

I grew up in a haunted house
Where the living were the ghosts.
Moths in cereal boxes.
A sickly-sweet humidity in the air.
We haunted our own bedrooms.
Roamed the halls at night.
Bumping into each other's secrets.
Never remembering to turn on a light.
Watched our parents give up and hide.
Turned the TV up louder
When they would fight.
Each day I would leave, passing through our white picket fence
Pretending to be different than who I was.
But a ghost child never forgets.

Cutting strings

I turned into a ghost.
Raised by your hands to sink into your dark.
Comfort found in silent compliance
While the rage simmered in my body.
Never could feel free from your endless
Marionette strings.
And at 30 years old, I grew into my heart.
Dove into the fear.
Looked the rage in the eyes.
I shook but I stayed.
Did what you couldn't, wouldn't do.
Heard the grief speak.
Let it scream until my tears ran clear.
This is my story, and I will tell it.
Your crocodile tears will not prevent it.
Only I tried to become until I became.
You do not know who I am anymore
Because I am not you.

F*ck being good

I just wanted to be a daughter
Not a substitute for your pain.
I just needed to be a child
Not a performer for your love.

Born with your burdens already on my shoulders
I carried your luggage for so long.
But I'm traveling much lighter these days.
I do not miss having to shove myself aside
In order to feel safe.

I will not be good
When I can be true.
I will not be good
To appease you.

Inner child

Oh, my beloved, those tired eyes.
The ones I catch in the mirror before they hide.
The daydreaming, the childish lies.
I wish you could remember how hard I try to keep you safe.
I know sometimes you think to search for me.
But how often it is that you believe you are alone.
Oh, my beloved, you had such a long day.
It's not that your feet ache.
It's a soul ache.
A goddamn soul ache.

Blackout

This blind rage.
Quick, turn the page.
I want to believe nothing matters.
But I'm red hot, seeing spots.
Back in different days, seeing different faces.
When it's yours I'm yelling at.

You are the mother I couldn't get away from.
The father who wouldn't stay.
All the adults who took something from a child.
All those fucking endless days.

I don't even recognize your face
Until I go away.
Shake off that other time and place.
I'm sorry that I am this way.
Everything matters inside this
Blackout place.

Tired youth

Too many ghosts inside my head.
Dancing behind my eyelids.
Always when I'm trying to stop the ache.
I could've been a dancer.
Wanted to sing.
I could've loved more.
Made more mistakes.
Could do all these things I suppose, still.
When did the hope of youth change?

Unconscious

There have been many times in my life
When I would go too far to feel alive.
Walking on the solid yellow line
Waiting to move until I'm staring down headlights.
Outdrinking all my friends.
Searching for a spark to ignite until early morning light.
Never finding happiness but I'd try again every night.
Chasing anyone who said they couldn't love me.
Always proving them right.
I found that instead of sitting still with myself
I could set my demons on fire
And use them as a guide.
Sometimes I wish I could go back
And give my younger self a hand to hold.
And a flashlight.
Or maybe just tell her
I'm waiting for her to find me.
She's safe and she'll be alright.

What i'd say to myself at twenty-one

That's not you.
That's who you think you need to be
In order to feel normal.

Because your heart always races
And you don't know why.
You don't know yet about everything
Your mind has chosen to hide.
But you know drinking
And putting yourself in risky situations
Makes you feel better.
Makes you feel alive.

You're keeping secrets.
From your friends.
From yourself too.
You don't like who you are
But you act too cool.
Your curated edges hurt the people
Who try to get to know you.

I see you.
I'm looking at you now in the bathroom mirror.
Know it's been a while but I still feel you all the time.
Know how much fun you have silencing your heart
But I promise it feels so much better letting it scream out loud.

You'll figure out why your heart races.
You'll learn to slow it down.
Your mind will learn to trust you
And you'll finally come out.
Because I know right now
Being anything except straight isn't something
You can think about.

You'll allow people to get to know you
And stop pretending you don't care.
And the people you choose as family
Are always there.

I can't wait for you to get here.
You're going to be so proud.

Detached

It is a gift.
It is a curse.
To be able to float away.
To take your mind somewhere safe.

Sometimes I go to a field of flowers.
Running through them wildly
In a pastel yellow dress.
The grass whipping past my knees.
It feels like a time I lived in before.
When my name was different
But my fire, the same.

Sometimes I go to the stage.
Singing out to strangers
That're screaming my name.
It feels like the person I would've been
If I hadn't forgotten my voice.

And sometimes I just float above my body.
Watching it take deep breaths.
Because sometimes it forgets
How to breathe.

ADHD tornado

The chaos of a mind.
Waking up every morning
In a tornado of time.
Speeding up.
Slowing down.
Up and down.
Round and round.
Watching my life play out
From behind stage curtains.
Until it's over and I'm spit out from whirling clouds.
Exhausted from the unproductive productivity.
At night I'll swear that I'll do better tomorrow.
I'll plan out every moment of the day.
Lull myself into a complacent sleep.
And in this sleep, I'll dream of dreamy things.
Until a tornado wakes me up.

Unheavy illness

I remember the first time anxiety
Decided it needed to drive.
I was five.
Sitting on the rug in preschool
Surrounded by other children.
I had recently begun my long career as a people pleaser.
Being good, behaving myself in order to be loved.
And I dug my fingers into my skin.
Because what I was feeling was so big
And I, so small.

I remember the first time
I had a panic attack.
I was thirteen.
Sitting in school surrounded by my classmates.
I thought, "I must be dying, and no one knows."
After it was over, I looked around wondering
If anyone else had noticed the shift in the air.
And I dug my fingers into my skin.
Because I had no idea what a panic attack was
But I knew I had to be damaged.

I remember the first time I decided
It was time to end my life.
I was a few weeks shy of sixteen.
Surrounded by people at a fancy party.
Watching them from outside my body.
Drinking and dancing in slow motion.
Acutely aware peace and a quiet mind were so close.
I just needed to get up, walk out the door.
Leave everything behind.

That was when I met my nephew's eyes.
Still only a baby, he held my gaze.
I stood there for what felt like hours.
His newness.
His innocence.
His unstained life.

I couldn't leave.
Wouldn't be a person he only knew from pictures.
So, I dug my fingers into my skin and sat back down.
Saddled with what to do now.
How do I make this bearable?
Where do I put the pain?

I am thirty-one now.
And I have experienced my share of
Anxiety, panic attacks and thoughts of ending my life.
But now I know anxiety by her name.
Why she shows up and how to listen to her
When she has something to say.
Sometimes she still demands to drive.
And although I prefer her safely buckled in the backseat
She still has ways of grabbing the keys.

But now I think life is beautiful
And I don't want to leave.
Because I am living it for myself
And working through the heavy pain.
Setting it down slowly, standing straighter every day.

And I am free.
I am free.

Father

Did you always know you were different?
I wish you had told me
Because
I am different too.
I hope one day it won't be seen that way.
Still, I know it's so much better now than
When you were young.
So, I understand why you felt you couldn't
Be openly free, in front of me.

Mom always said I have her father's eyes.
But I've begun to think I have yours.
Sometimes, when I catch them in the mirror
I see a flash of you.
Wild, endless pools.
Lines underneath from too much fun.

I know what it feels like to desperately need
To be free.
I just wish you had handled it differently.
I felt like a part of a secret.
A cover for your shame.
You weren't there for me.
But I'm older now
And there for myself.
I know it must make you happy that
Now we are both free.

Boundless

A magical life.
Kissing girls and holding hands
Under the trees.
My sweet love with his intense eyes
And gentle smile.
He's always for me, a magical thing.
My forever ring sitting pretty on my finger.
Our love is whatever we want it to be.
We are free.
And I like strolling in the woods with a girl
In a golden dress.
Dropping flowers at her feet.
Every time she meets my gaze
I don't breathe.
A divine creature.
She's always for me.
The power of three.
A trinity.

Golden

Golden sweater hanging on a tree.
She lays me gently down by the creek.
Desperate to have her hair fall down
And surround me.
To her, all my mistakes are wiped clean.
Bathed, born again.
In her eyes, I am seen.
Her slow smile.
I found my Sunday ceremony.
And I worship
Here in the grass holding her hand.

Dream girl

The smell of your strawberry blonde hair
Is so frustratingly
Distracting.
I could write a homily
On what you've done to me.
Some would call us heathens
Or sick.
For I only worship at your body.
Let them judge and let them stare.
I have spent far too long dreaming of you
To try to hide.
Take me to your favorite spot in your mind.
Where you keep who you really are.
Release her upon me.
And then we will go to dinner
As if my lips don't shine
Of you.

Inventing her

I am tempting.
I am tempted.
She knows.
She advances.
An apple balanced in her palm.
A beating heart score.
Her next move is my last view
Of everything in this room.
I am spellbound by her entirety.

Divine intervention

I'm not god.
He doesn't exist.
But I do.
And I'm god-like.
Pray to me, nightly.
Real flesh, flushed and soft.
Turns to water with a touch.
My god, my god, my god I'm so alive.
Don't say sorry.
Scream your delight.
I created this to enjoy.
I'm not the devil.
He doesn't exist.
But I do.
And I'm devil-like.
Eat the apple.
Devour it and lick the juice from your mouth.

Ungodly carnality

I find you in the garden.
Twirling an apple core in your hands.
A juicy grin spreads across your
Otherworldy face.
A total disregard for the moral ones
Ready to beat you down
With their judgmental tongues.
You stride on over to me.
Hook your fingers in my jeans.
No space in between.
A representation of what they say
Shouldn't be.
And yet we are here.
Basking in the sin of our bodies' love.

The chase

I hunted for you.
Tore through my gilded forest
To watch the fire, fill your eyes
When you realized
You had been caught.
You looked hot to the touch.
And feral.
That sacred evergreen path
Is where we feel safe to be our wounded animals.
As I imagined being loved by you
I heard the snap of a branch
As you stepped
Closer.

For P.J.R

He is a dream that I never thought
Would come to me.
A love told in the stars.
The one who never shamed me
For all of my scars.

No, I don't want you to leave.
Yes, I push you away.
Because my shadows whisper to me
"Why would he ever stay?"

He stays because he sees me.
It's a lesson I learn, new, everyday.
I can be loved for exactly as I am.

Sometimes I just watch him sleep.
Eyelashes grazing his kind face.
His chest rising and falling in blissful peace.
And even after all this time
He is magnificent to me.

Buried

Hey, brown eyes.
We have both buried so much.
Every time I think I have reached the bottom of you
You show me more.
Whatever you recover.
Whatever you reveal.
Whatever comes up for you to heal.
I'm right here beside you
With my own shovel.
To help when you are tired.
To dig myself out from my own
Self-inflicted landslide.

Remedy

Take me to the woods.
For I have never felt more seen
Than amongst an audience of trees.
Bring me to the ocean.
I want to scrub myself of all my sins.
A clean slate so that I can rack them up again.
Lay me down in a wildflower field.
Remind me there's hope and child-like joy.
Come and rest beside me.
I want to look at you
And remember people
Are made from stars.

We aren't at war with nature

If people could remember
They are as much part of nature
As an apple on a tree
Would they treat our mother differently?

If everyone could hear the cry
Of a mother cow when her baby is taken
Would they continue to let it happen?

If we were all lucky enough to lie in the grass
And stare up at the stars every night
Would we continue to feel
Like the most important parts in our world?

It's hard to be a person.
It's scary to have no control.
The pain in this world, gets to us all.
But the solution can't be to conquer and destroy
So that we don't feel so small.

Do you want to spend forever with me?

Court me in the cemetery.
Dying flowers on the graves.
We'll fall in love slowly, it's the best pace.
Days of dreams, years of age.
And when it's time to rest our bones
We'll return to where our love first became.
You'll pluck a rose off a loney grave.
Beauty even in death, love even in pain.

Autumn dreams

I want to live inside October.
Learn all there is to know about her.
Why she sets herself on fire.
A most exquisite death.
Tell her it's only with her I can breathe.
A crisp bite of her apple.
I revere, I worship
Her.

Please, don't hurt me

I am but a jack-o-lantern.
Hollowed out but smiling.
Or is it a grimace?
Can you ever tell?
I'll share a secret.
It's a snarl.
And I have sharp teeth.
Stay far from me.

Masking

Is it Halloween?
Are you wearing that mask for me?
Desperate, I try to stare through.
I only want to see what is underneath.
See, I wear a mask too.
I'm not sure I ever take it off.
Hiding from myself too.
I know that you are tired.
We could go into a room.
Take off our masks
And scream.

See through

Crushed velvet.
Crushed petals between your teeth.
This is it, my fantasy.
Where you think I'm cool
And you believe my mystery.
Lipstick-stained joint keeps me steady
Underneath your shiny, diamond stare.
This life would be so dull without
Creatures like you.
Because you don't want to know my mask.
Don't want to hear a please or a thank you
Come from my mouth.
You only want to seep into my skin.
Find my wounded animal.
And let her out.

You're cool, i'm dead

It fucks me up
To watch you dance.
It feels like you must be privy
To some of the Universe's secrets.
How else could you explain
Your UFO eyes
Keeping me in a trance.

It blows my heart up
To make a fool of myself.
I can't take the shame.
Especially when I can feel your eyes on my brain.

I am both terrified
And electrified
That you know I'm on the planet.
How about Tuesday, you pant.
You could come over, fall into my gravity.

House party trip

Fever dreams.
Everything that I want to come to me
Runs down my face for you to read.
My dripping conscience got on your new sweater.
Now you can't meet my starless eyes.
I never know why I'm here.
This dizzy party.
This punch-drunk life.
I hand you back your heart key.
I wish to memorize your mind.
But I get lost every time.
I think I just need to lie down.
Outline my body in chalk.
Save some time.

Unyielding

What are you going to do with that passion you have?
I've seen it flicker behind your eyes.
Smelled your desperation to let it
Burn down your polite walls.
I know what the world has done to you.
For they do it to us all.
I had to root myself in my darkness
In order to release the gag they had in my mouth.
I want to hear your voice
In agony.
In anger.
In pleasure.
In harmony.
Show me the darkness you've held back.
Because, my beloved, they are wrong.
You are not chaos.
You are power.

Wild

I came when the trees burned.
I left when they were all dead.
You tried to love me.
I loved the world instead.
Cause the way it turns attracts me like a light.
And the darkness keeps me warm at night.
I just want to live my life, honest.
And I just want to live my life
Wild.

Pretend love

I get stoned to think of you.
It's the only time my mind is quiet enough
To find you inside.
Moonlight skin.
Ocean nights.
It's been a while since I took the dive.
I remember your whisper
Reminding me no one could know what we did.
Fixing your shirt in the car.
Looking away, I was already so far.
"Time to Pretend" coming on the radio.
How ironic, I thought.
Fated to pretend that this meant less than it did.

To be new

Walk me into January.
A New Years babe.
I'm bathed and renewed.
All my faults are art I'll learn to frame.
December is for remembering mistakes.
January, we walk into something new.
I want to be there with you.

Advice to the mirror

For someone so young
So vibrant
So seemingly free
You seem to know time so well.
Like old, old friends.
What happened to you?
Tell me, what's on your heart?
Cheer up, love.
It will be fun again.
There will be joy simply because there is pain.
They go hand in hand.
Like old, old friends.
Hey, stop giving yourself away
To endlessly hungry black holes.
They don't know your soul.
It will be fun again.
There will be dancing
Under the moon to Stevie.
Invite all your real friends to the reverie.
The ones who always encouraged you
To let go, throw your head back and howl.

Love me, love my ghosts

You'll always have ghosts.
Sometimes, you'll be one yourself.
You'll recognize it in others too.
And you'll have to let them float away
For a while.

But they'll come back
Once they befriend themselves
And all their ghosts.

Because they show you
How you really feel
And point you to what needs to heal
I'll always make room
For all my ghosts.

Fin.

About the author

Shaelyn Rhiannon does in fact love the band Fleetwood Mac. Now that that's out of the way... *Inviting all the Ghosts to Dinner* is Shaelyn's first poetry collection. Well, her first published one. She has been writing poems, lyrics, and stories since she first learned to write. She hopes to continue to live out her childhood dream for many years to come. She is currently traveling the U.S. as a full time RVer with her two dogs, one cat, and one husband. She recommends keeping it to one husband while on the road but does think adding another cat could work.